BIBLE PROMISES

GIVEN TO

Elizabeth Sabrina Forbes

ON THIS DATE

5/4/98

BY

Maw Maw Rinda

BIBLE PROMISES

SAM BUTCHER

Thomas Nelson, Inc.
Nashville

Scripture quotations noted CEV are from
THE CONTEMPORARY ENGLISH VERSION. © 1991
by the American Bible Society. Used by permission.
Scripture quotations noted ICB are from
The International Children's Bible, New Century Version,
Copyright © 1986, 1988 by Word Publishing.
Used by permission.

Library of Congress Cataloging-in-Publication Data

Bible. English. Contemporary English. Selections. 1997.
    Precious moments Bible promises / [illustrated by] Sam Butcher.
        p.   cm.
    Summary: A collection of verses from the Contemporary English Version
and the International Children's Bible, New Century Version, grouped by the
topics of "Peace," "Mercy," and "Love."
    ISBN 0-8499-1463-9
    1. Bible—Illustrations. 2. God—Promises—Biblical teaching—Juvenile
literature. [1. Bible—Selections.] I. Butcher, Samuel J. (Samuel John). 1939- ill.
II. Bible. English. International Children's Bible. Selections. 1997. III. Title.
BS560 1997
220.5'208—dc21 —dc21
[220.5'208]   97-27093
                                                  CIP
                                                  AC

Printed in the United States of America.

97 98 99 00 01 02 03 RRD 9 8 7 6 5 4 3 2 1

CONTENTS

INTRODUCTION

In all of Sam Butcher's work, there is a connection between the names of the figurines and the verses in the Bible. It is evident that Sam's faith inspired the creation of the Precious Moments® illustrations.

In this book, Sam shares the complete Bible verses that inspired the Precious Moments® art and figurines. It is his hope that the peace and understanding that he has experienced through these Bible texts will become your joy as well.

PEACE

A GREAT REWARD

God blesses those people who make peace. They will be called his children! God blesses those people who are treated badly for doing right. They belong to the kingdom of heaven.... Be happy and excited! You will have a great reward in heaven. People did these same things to the prophets who lived long ago.

MATTHEW 5:9–10, 12 CEV

God blesses those
people who make peace.

BE READY!

Put on all the armor that God gives, so you can defend yourself against the devil's tricks.... Be ready! Let the truth be like a belt around your waist, and let God's justice protect you like armor. Your desire to tell the good news about peace should be like shoes on your feet. Let your faith be like a shield, and you will be able to stop all the flaming arrows of the evil one. Let God's saving power be like a helmet, and for a sword use God's message that comes from the Spirit. Never stop praying, especially for others. Always pray by the power of the Spirit. Stay alert and keep praying for God's people.

EPHESIANS 6:11, 14–18 CEV

Put on all the
armor that God gives.

THE LORD IS GOOD!

Shout praises to the LORD, everyone on this earth. Be joyful and sing as you come in to worship the LORD! You know the LORD is God! He created us, and we belong to him; we are his people, the sheep in his pasture. Be thankful and praise the LORD as you enter his temple. The LORD is good! His love and faithfulness will last forever.

PSALM 100 CEV

Shout praises
to the Lord.

HE IS HOLY

Praise the Lord, you angels. Praise the Lord's glory and power. Praise the Lord for the glory of his name. Worship the Lord because he is holy.... The Lord gives strength to his people. The Lord blesses his people with peace.

PSALM 29: 1–2, 11 ICB

Praise the Lord's
glory and power.

MERCY

EVERYTHING I NEED

The Lord is my shepherd. I have everything I need.
He gives me rest in green pastures. He leads me to
calm water. He gives me new strength. For the good
of his name, he leads me on paths that are right.
Even if I walk through a very dark valley, I will not
be afraid because you are with me. Your rod and
your walking stick comfort me. You prepare a meal
for me in front of my enemies. You pour oil on my
head. You give me more than I can hold. Surely
your goodness and love will be with me all my life.
And I will live in the house of the Lord forever.

PSALM 23 ICB

The Lord
is my shepherd.

REST FOR YOUR SOULS

"Come to me, all of you who are tired and have heavy loads. I will give you rest. Accept my work and learn from me. I am gentle and humble in spirit. And you will find rest for your souls. The work that I ask you to accept is easy. The load I give you to carry is not heavy."

MATTHEW 11:28–30 ICB

The work that I ask you to accept is easy.
The load I give you to carry is not heavy.

NOTHING CAN SEPARATE US FROM GOD'S LOVE

So what should we say about this? If God is with us, then no one can defeat us…. Can anything separate us from the love Christ has for us? Can troubles or problems or sufferings? If we have no food or clothes, if we are in danger, or even if death comes—can any of these things separate us from Christ's love?… Yes, I am sure that nothing can separate us from the love God has for us. Not death, not life, not angels, not ruling spirits, nothing now, nothing in the future, no powers, nothing above us, nothing below us, or anything else in the whole world will ever be able to separate us from the love of God that is in Christ Jesus our Lord.

ROMANS 8:31, 35, 38–39 ICB

If God is with us,
then no one can defeat us.

GOD WILL TAKE CARE OF YOU

Trust the Lord and do good. Live in the land and enjoy its safety. Enjoy serving the Lord. And he will give you what you want. Depend on the Lord. Trust him, and he will take care of you. Then your goodness will shine like the sun. Your fairness will shine like the noonday sun.... In a little while there will be no more wicked people. You may look for them, but they will be gone. People who are not proud will inherit the land. They will enjoy complete peace.

PSALM 37:3–6, 10–11 ICB

Trust the Lord.

THE LIGHT
THAT GIVES LIFE

Once again Jesus spoke to the people. This time he said, "I am the light for the world! Follow me, and you won't be walking in the dark. You will have the light that gives life."

JOHN 8:12 CEV

I am the light for the world.

AT NIGHT WE MAY CRY...

I will praise you, LORD! You saved me from the grave and kept my enemies from celebrating my death. I prayed to you, LORD God, and you healed me, saving me from death and the grave. Your faithful people, LORD, will praise you with songs and honor your holy name. Your anger lasts a little while, but your kindness lasts for a lifetime. At night we may cry, but when morning comes we will celebrate.... I will never stop singing your praises, my LORD and my God.

PSALM 30:1–5, 12 CEV

When morning
comes we will celebrate.

LOVE

IF I DO NOT HAVE LOVE...

I may speak in different languages of men or even angels. But if I do not have love, then I am only a noisy bell or a ringing cymbal. I may have the gift of prophecy; I may understand all the secret things of God and all knowledge; and I may have faith so great that I can move mountains. But even with all these things, if I do not have love, then I am nothing.... Love is patient and kind. Love is not jealous, it does not brag, and it is not proud.

1 Corinthians 13:1–2, 4 ICB

Love is patient and kind.

LOVE ALWAYS CONTINUES STRONG

Love is not rude, is not selfish, and does not become angry easily. Love does not remember wrongs done against it. Love is not happy with evil, but is happy with the truth. Love patiently accepts all things. It always trusts, always hopes, and always continues strong.

1 CORINTHIANS 13:5–7 ICB

Love patiently
accepts all things.

LOVE AS I HAVE LOVED YOU

"This is my command: Love each other as I have loved you.... You are my friends if you do what I command you.... You did not choose me; I chose you. And I gave you this work, to go and produce fruit. I want you to produce fruit that will last. Then the Father will give you anything you ask for in my name. This is my command: Love each other."

JOHN 15:12, 14, 16–17 ICB

Love each other.

GO IN A GENTLE WAY

Brothers, someone in your group might do something wrong. You who are spiritual should go to him and help make him right again. You should do this in a gentle way.... Help each other with your troubles. When you do this, you truly obey the law of Christ.

GALATIANS 6:1–2 ICB

Help each other
with your troubles.

WHEN YOU ARE ANGRY, DO NOT SIN

In the Lord's name, I tell you this. I warn you: Do not continue living like those who do not believe. Their thoughts are worth nothing.... So you must stop telling lies. Tell each other the truth because we all belong to each other in the same body. When you are angry, do not sin. And do not go on being angry all day. Do not give the devil a way to defeat you.

Ephesians 4:17, 25–27 icb

Do not go on
being angry all day.

A BIG HARVEST

Remember this saying, "A few seeds make a small harvest, but a lot of seeds make a big harvest." Each of you must make up your own mind about how much to give. But don't feel sorry that you must give and don't feel that you are forced to give. God loves people who love to give.

2 CORINTHIANS 9:6–7 CEV

God loves people
who love to give.

GIFTS THAT CONTINUE

Love never ends. There are gifts of prophecy, but they will be ended. There are gifts of speaking in different languages, but those gifts will end. There is the gift of knowledge, but it will be ended. These things will end, because this knowledge and these prophecies we have are not complete. But when perfection comes, the things that are not complete will end.... So these three things continue forever: faith, hope and love. And the greatest of these is love.

1 Corinthians 13:8–10, 13 icb

Love never ends.